RONA MUNRO

Rona Munro has written extensively for stage, radio, film and television including the recent adaptations of *My Name Is Lucy Barton* for the Bridge Theatre, London and Manhattan Theatre Company on Broadway, New York, and *Captain Corelli's Mandolin* for Neil Laidlaw Productions. She wrote the award-winning trilogy *The James Plays* for the National Theatre of Scotland, the National Theatre of Great Britain and the Edinburgh International Festival. This is the sixth play in that series about the medieval history of Scotland. The fourth, *James IV: Queen of the Fight*, premiered at the Festival Theatre, Edinburgh, in 2022, produced by Raw Material and Capital Theatres in association with the National Theatre of Scotland.

Other credits include award-winning plays *Iron* for the Traverse Theatre and Royal Court London, *The Maiden Stone* for Hampstead Theatre, *Little Eagles* and *The Indian Boy* for the Royal Shakespeare Company, and *Bold Girls* for 7:84 Theatre Scotland.

Film and TV work includes *Oranges and Sunshine*, directed by Jim Loach and starring Emily Watson and Hugo Weaving, the Ken Loach film *Ladybird, Ladybird*, which won a Silver Bear at the Berlin Festival, *Aimée & Jaguar*, a Silver Bear winner and Golden Globe nomination, and BAFTA nominated *Bumping the Odds* for the BBC. She has also written many other single plays for TV and contributed to series such as *Doctor Who*.

Other Titles in this Series

Rona Munro

MARY

NICK HERN BOOKS

London

www.nickhernbooks.co.uk

A Nick Hern Book

Mary first published in Great Britain as a paperback original in 2022 by Nick Hern Books Limited, The Glasshouse, 49a Goldhawk Road, London W12 8QP

Mary copyright © 2022 Rona Munro

Cover image: n9design.com; photography by Aliaksei Kaponia via Shutterstock

Designed and typeset by Nick Hern Books, London
Printed in Great Britain by Mimeo Ltd, Huntingdon, Cambridgeshire PE29 6XX

A CIP catalogue record for this book is available from the British Library

ISBN 978 1 83904 1 334

Woodland
CARBON
www.woodlandcarbon.co.uk
NICK HERN BOOKS
Printed on Carbon Captured paper

Mary was first performed at Hampstead Theatre, London, on 31 October 2022, with the following cast:

JAMES MELVILLE   Douglas Henshall
AGNES   Rona Morison
THOMPSON   Brian Vernel

Director   Roxana Silbert
Designer   Ashley Martin-Davis
Lighting   Matt Haskins
Composer and Sound   Nick Powell
Movement   Ayse Tashkiran
Casting   Helena Palmer CDG
Assistant Director   Marlie Haco

Author's Note
Rona Munro

This play, *Mary*, is the sixth instalment in the cycle of plays I've written about the medieval Stuart monarchs of Scotland: *The James Plays*. At the time of writing this introduction, the fourth instalment, *James IV: The Queen of the Fight*, has just started a Scottish tour, produced by Raw Material and Capital Theatres. The next instalment, chronologically, would cover the reign of James V, but while that play (*Katherine*) is now completed, *Mary* was written first and has already found a production, at Hampstead Theatre.

The reason this story was more urgently in my imagination was that I had already, years ago, done extensive research into the stories of the reign of Mary Queen of Scots. I already had a strong and, I'd claim, well-informed opinion about the events at the end of her reign. It's not an opinion all historians share but, if you sift through original sources and eyewitness accounts of the time, I struggle to see how you can draw any other conclusion. I think Mary Queen of Scots was raped by James Hepburn, Earl of Bothwell, to force her into a marriage that briefly gave him power but ultimately destroyed them both.

What happened between Mary and Bothwell is a story that has, I think, great contemporary resonance. Women's narratives have often been twisted to serve other interests and destroy their true experience. History gaslights women because, until very recently, history was written by men. At the time what happened to Mary was spun as a story of unwise lust and passion, a love story between Mary and Bothwell that confirmed she was unfit to rule. It's easy to see why it was spun that way in 1567, as it very much served the interest of those grabbing for power. What's less forgivable, to me, is how some later historians have bought into that version of events without re-examining them with empathy and with the greater cultural understanding we now have on the nature of consent.

There are probably thousands of versions of Mary's story and everyone, including me, has used her as a vivid vehicle for their own favoured narrative. The story of how powerful women, or indeed any woman, can be manipulated, abused, and terrorised by sexual violence has been told many times, and should be told many more. However, there's another story I don't feel I've seen so often, the story of why decent, caring, moral men – the majority of the male population, I'd say – still tolerate and enable that violence. James Melville was, I think, such a man. I believe he did love Mary, but he allowed the events we see in the play. I wanted to try to tell the story of that moral journey. For me, that has the greatest contemporary resonance. What Mary faced is not nearly as different from what any woman might face now as we might like to imagine.

I used Melville's memoirs to get a sense of his character and to tell the story, in its details, as he tells it. However, the character of Melville in the play amalgamates the experience of other men who were originally loyal companions to Mary, and I've used other eyewitness accounts to provide the details of the narrative.

Agnes and Thompson, the two other characters in the play, are fictional. However, their goals and attitudes reflect two contrasting interest groups in Scotland at this time of upheaval: one that is quite hard-line, informed by the potential of the religious revolution; one which is more pragmatic, and about maintaining power for the men who already have it.

What happened to Mary, though unarguably rape, in my opinion, may not have been as brutal as I describe, but Bothwell's assault was witnessed – and what I describe reflects what happened to her, over and over, in all imaginations after that assault was made public.

Whatever your opinion on the necessity of reform of the Church in Scotland at this time, or whatever egalitarian good we can claim from that Reformation, it came at this price.

I don't ever presume to have answers, only relevant questions, but I do think that cost bears examination.

There is a poem I wrote to be used in the first production. It tries to echo songs we know existed at the time: apparently sweet, melodic ballads that were actually vicious slanders aimed at Mary. A mermaid was another word for a whore. Earl Bothwell's family crest carried a hare. So this song, 'The Mermaid and the Hare', carries that subtext. Its use is optional in any production but included for interest.

> The hare rins oer the bonny green,
> Tae spy the siller sea,
> The mermaid stands ahint the wave –
> 'Cam oer the strand tae me.'
>
> 'I cannae swim yon siller sea,
> Nor you walk oer the green.'
> But she has rin frae sea tae strand –
> A hare micht wed a queen.

Glossary of Scots Words

Siller – silver
Ahint – behind
Strand – beach
Rin – run
Mich – might

Characters

JAMES MELVILLE, *a courtier and officer of Scottish Government, mid-thirties to mid-fifties*
THOMPSON, *a servant of court and government, mid-twenties*
AGNES, *a servant of the royal household, mid-twenties*

This text went to press before the end of rehearsals and so may differ slightly from the play as performed.

Outside a Room in Holyrood Palace

This is April 1567 but it could be any time.

A public area in Holyrood Palace.

THOMPSON *is on the floor. He's been beaten, viciously. He's bleeding, trying to pull himself together.*

JAMES *comes in. He stops dead, taking in the carnage.*

JAMES. Oh you'll need to shift, man, you canny lie about here.

THOMPSON *can't answer, struggling to sit up.*

After a moment, JAMES *goes to help him.*

Alright?

Can you get up?

THOMPSON *tries, with* JAMES*'s help,* JAMES *supports him on his feet.*

Wait here a minute. You'll be good in a minute.

THOMPSON *has to lean on him.* JAMES *sees that the other man has bled on him.*

Oh… shite…

Blood…

You're bleeding on my jaiket there… Can you…?

He fumbles for a handkerchief. Gives it to THOMPSON.

It's just it's new so…

THOMPSON *mops at his face.*

THOMPSON (*re: the hanky*). Thank you.

JAMES. Nae bother.

Keep it.

THOMPSON *is still trying to give it back.*

(*A little impatient.*) Keep it! Keep it.

Can you shift yoursel? Can you walk?

It's clear THOMPSON *can't.*

She's coming through. I don't want her to see you.

You'll frighten her. She musn't see you. Come on now.

He closes the doors.

Oh! Bit of help here?

Right. You can stay here till you're no bleeding everywhere.

THOMPSON. She needs to see me. She needs to see what he's done to me.

JAMES is still quiet but very firm.

JAMES. No. You'll frighten her. And she's been frightened enough already. Alright?

JAMES sees they've left a trail of blood.

Aw fuck's sake.

He hurries over, trying to clean it up. It's beyond him.

AGNES, *a palace servant, is hurrying past engaged in some errand.* JAMES *calls to her.*

AGNES *checks, sees the blood and* THOMPSON.

AGNES (*shocked, quiet*). Mother of God...

JAMES. Come on. Quick now!

AGNES indicates off.

AGNES. But the Queen...

JAMES (*cutting her off*). Will no be looking round and missing you. Get something to clean this mess up.

As AGNES *hesitates.*

She canny see this!

AGNES *hurries off*. JAMES *goes back to* THOMPSON.

Who did this?

THOMPSON. Who do you think?

JAMES. Bothwell.

THOMPSON *says nothing, struggling with pain*.

Was it Bothwell?

THOMPSON. Of course it was fucking Bothwell!

JAMES (*stern*). Keep it down!

Alright.

Alright.

First things first.

How did you make this happen?

THOMPSON. *Make* this happen? You're putting this on me?!

JAMES. How long have you been part of the household here?

THOMPSON. Two months but...

JAMES (*cutting him off*). So you've seen Bothwell. You've seen what he's like?

THOMPSON. Aye but...

JAMES. So you were in a room with Earl Bothwell, close enough to talk to him, close enough for him to hear you, and you said...?

THOMPSON *doesn't reply*.

What did you say to him?

THOMPSON. I didny say it to him.

JAMES. What did you say, in his hearing?

THOMPSON. They were talking about protecting the Queen...

JAMES (*prompts*). And?

THOMPSON. I just said it to the boy on the door with me.

JAMES. You said?

THOMPSON. If they want to keep her safe from murderers she might want to look for a different Captain of the Guard.

JAMES. And the Captain of her Guard, Bothwell, heard you.

THOMPSON. He heard folk laugh.

JAMES. That'd do it. But you're alive. So anarchy isny our ruler yet. No quite yet. Christ.

JAMES *is thinking.*

AGNES *is back with water to clean* THOMPSON *up. She starts doing this.*

JAMES *comes out of his reverie and notices her.*

Where's the Queen now?

AGNES. She's in her chapel, praying, again.

JAMES. Good. We've got a bit of time before she comes through then. Did you bring this boy anything for his pain?

AGNES. Like what?

JAMES *sighs. He gets out a hip flask and gives it to* THOMPSON.

THOMPSON *drinks gratefully, passes it back.*

JAMES. Keep it. So you're new here, eh? When did you say you got here?

THOMPSON. Couple of months ago.

JAMES. So who's looking out for you? Who're you working for?

THOMPSON (*daft question*). I'm in the Queen's household, same as you.

JAMES. Christ, you're green. You've no even grown up out the mud far enough to look around, eh?

(*Sudden new thought.*) Whoa! Hud on...

(*To* THOMPSON.) They were talking about protecting her?

THOMPSON. Aye.

JAMES. What do they mean, protecting her?

She's leaving, today, for Stirling.

THOMPSON *says nothing.*

They mean to stop her leaving?

Still nothing – yes they do.

Who's in charge of the boys on the gate?

Nothing from THOMPSON *– he's on the gate.*

(*Realising.*) You are. You're on the gate.

Well, you need to let her ride through. You need to tell your men to let us ride through. They can't *stop* us!? That's… She's the Queen, she canny be stopped.

Nothing from THOMPSON.

What's your name?

THOMPSON. Thompson.

JAMES. And you're no attached to any of the lords?

THOMPSON. Moray sent to my father for young men he could trust.

JAMES. Well, the Earl of Moray's away to France, isn't he? So who have you attached yourself to in the meantime?

THOMPSON *says nothing.*

Christ save you, you're adrift. Alright. I'll pay you. I'll see you right.

THOMPSON. I get…

I'm part of the household. I get paid.

JAMES. You canny live off that. Look around you. Who's living off that?

AGNES. Me.

JAMES. There you go.

(*Indicates* AGNES.) You want to end up like her?

THOMPSON *still doesn't respond.*

Seriously, man! You know who I am? You're turning down my patronage?

THOMPSON. I think I need to keep the gate shut.

JAMES. I see. I see. Well, you're the boy that knows which way the wind's blowing, eh? You've got the finger on the pulse of power. Two months. Wow. You've got it all worked out, eh?

THOMPSON. I think the Queen needs to stay here.

JAMES. Why do you think that, though?

(*New tack.*) What do you think is at stake here?

What happened this February just gone? Anything significant? Anything catch your attention?

THOMPSON *is sulky and silent.*

Come on! Say it. You need to hear yourself say it.

THOMPSON. The murder.

JAMES. Aye.

They killed the Queen's husband.

(*Lowering his voice.*) Bothwell had the Queen's husband killed. You *know* that! Everyone knows that.

AGNES. And we know why he did it.

JAMES *spares her a glance.*

JAMES. No, you know fuck-all so shut up.

(*To* THOMPSON.) Is that the violent chaos you think should get hold of our Queen?

So why are you doing this?

THOMPSON. Because that's what...

(*Struggling to explain this for a moment*.) Do you know how many of the great lords of Scotland were in that room?

JAMES. I could take a guess.

THOMPSON. Well. There you go. They want the gate to stay shut.

JAMES (*scoffs*). 'Great lords', what's great about them?

Bothwell's got a great army round him. That's what should have your attention. You think she should stay here, with him, and all the servants who jump to murder whenever he whistles?

You'll take the orders of a roomful of cowards over Mary Stuart's? She's your *Queen*!

Where's Bothwell now?

THOMPSON. I don't know. He took himself off after...

JAMES (*cutting in*)....After he'd flattened you. As long as he stays in Edinburgh.

He breaks off as he sees AGNES, *moving away.*

Where do you think you're going?!

She stops.

Where are you going?

AGNES. You think I'm yours to command, do you?

JAMES. Sorry... who the *fuck* are you?

AGNES. Agnes Turnbull. No?

Well, my father was huntsman to the Queen's father, my grandmother served the old Queen in her chamber, I was called to service in the palace when *you* wereny even here, my lord, so...

THOMPSON (*cutting over this*). She speaks. On the high street. Have you not seen her?

JAMES (*irrelevant*). Why the fuck would I be wandering up the high street to watch some bold-faced lassie doing a turn?

THOMPSON (*enthused*). She talks about the new Protestant faith. She preaches...

AGNES (*cutting in, correcting*). No, no, I dinny dae that. Knox and others wi' better voices than me can preach, I just gather the army to march behind them...

JAMES (*cutting her off*). Aye, aye! I'm sure it's great entertainment. I'll get mysel in the front row, next chance I have. Meantime you stay *here*, missus!

He blocks her way to any exit.

There's no one you need to go and talk to, is there?

AGNES. You canny make me...

JAMES (*cutting her off*). Aye. I can.

(*To* THOMPSON, *trying a different tone.*) Son, this is going to turn around. The wheel will turn. The wheel always turns. A canny man sees it moving and gets himself onto the half going up while the rest goes doon. So you get that gate open, you come to me in a few weeks...

THOMPSON. I can't do that.

That's not...

Those are no my orders.

JAMES. Well, you better take your orders from me now, eh? That's what you need to be doing. You can see that. Eh?

AGNES. Aye, you're wanting out the gate but you're nae taking him wi' you. Are you?

He's already taken a beating. You want them to kill him?

A beat.

JAMES. Good point.

Aye... aye... good point, well made.

Fuck you.

(*To* THOMPSON.) Alright then, how long have I got?

THOMPSON. Eh?

JAMES. Before they come for the Queen.

THOMPSON. I dinny think they'll come for her, they just...

   Well, we've to let them know if she asks to go through the
   gate. And it's to stay shut.

JAMES (*quiet, firm*). We'll be heading out with bags and
   baggage before it's dark and that's no one's business but
   your Queen's.

   (*Brisk*.) Right then! It ay comes down to love or money.
   Everything on earth. You're no after my money... and as the
   lady here has so eloquently reminded us there are risks, to all
   of us, who love the Queen...

AGNES. What about the love of God?

JAMES. Eh?

AGNES. You said everything on earth comes down to love or
   money. What about the love of God?

JAMES. Well, is that no love?

   Excuse me but I'm talking to Thompson here! I don't need to
   persuade you, do I?

AGNES. Mebbe you do.

JAMES. How's that?

THOMPSON. She's saying what everyone's saying.

JAMES. Which is?

AGNES. That your Queen's a murderous long stripe o' hoor
   that kisses the Pope's arse and would sell Scotland back to
   Rome if she could.

JAMES. Wow.

   I could probably have you killed. You do know that.

AGNES. On you go! Try it!

JAMES. So tempting.

(*Controls himself.*) She's no selling Scotland to anyone. If she wanted to do that we'd all be sitting here speaking French, which is my favoured language by the way, better for polite conversation altogether.

She does not kiss the Pope's arse. She keeps her faith and lets us keep ours.

(*Indicating himself, pointed.*) I'm as good a Protestant as either of you and I thank her for that wisdom. So might you when you've dug your manners out your arse.

Long stripe o' hoor.

I wouldny bandy the word hoor around, state o' you.

Murderous.

Murderous.

Where are you getting that?

AGNES. Where do you think?

JAMES. Who's she killed?

AGNES. The father of her bairn.

JAMES. Darnley? Bothwell did that. Did we no just say…

AGNES (*cutting him off*). Because she telt him to!

JAMES. Do you know who your Queen is? I've known her since she was nine years old by the way. She's twenty-four now, fifteen years. Do you know what I've always known about her?

She's a motherless bairn.

A beat.

Look at you, look at your vicious wee suspicious faces. You've been gobbling lies like geese wi' grain, eh? Stuffed with them.

He takes a moment, thinking.

THOMPSON (*to* AGNES). Have you seen me? I try to get to the front. Have you seen me listening to you?

AGNES. Aye. Course I have.

THOMPSON. I didny know if you'd noticed me.

AGNES. Thompson, I'm no staying here because I'm feart o' this one. I'm here to watch over you.

JAMES (*driving over this*). Beautiful. Pick it up when we're no on the brink of bloody chaos, eh?

So Bothwell meets me on the stair. I'd heard Darnley had been killed and I'd come to see the Queen.

She didny know where to put hersel.

A ghost.

Bothwell meets me on my way out. God he's looking like a butcher's dog left locked in the meat store, eh? Canny keep the glee out his gaze. 'Strangest thing, James,' he says, picking up my name like I'd made him a present of it, 'Strangest thing. Young Darnley's lodgings were struck by lightning, but when we got there, the house had burnt up, but there's Darnley, lying deid under a tree, wi'oot a mark on him! Can you believe it?!' He says, and his eyes are twinkling with his bloody joke, 'Go up and look at his body if you dinny believe me, no a mark on him!'

And those eyes, 'Call me a liar then, go on, go *on*! I dare you!'

They wouldny let me look at the body, as it happens.

But I'm sure if someone's held your nose and stopped your mouth with his big gloved mitts while his boys held your arms and legs pinned, there wouldny be much of a mark on you. Bit of bruising maybe. I don't know. Like I said, I didny see the body. Poor boy was just in his sark, did you hear? Found wi' his pale naked arse oot his nightshirt. Terrible way to go. Not quick and you'd ken there was no mercy in those gloved fingers stopping your breath...

Bothwell was slapping his gloves on his hand while he talked to me.

I'll never know if he did the killing himsel. I do know he willny have done it alane... but... all of it was his.

There was no lightning of course. They blew up the house with gunpowder.

A murdering devil. Clear.

It was always clear. Don't you think so? Anyone could see that in him. Well... look at the state of you, eh?

Know what *she* says about him?

'He looks rough but he's got a good heart.' Aye. She thinks he's an ugly guard dog. A lovable, toothless bear.

She's a motherless bairn. She smiles at the world and hopes that's enough to make it smile back.

She's a toddler sitting in the lion's open mouth, giggling about how sparkly its teeth are.

AGNES. The assize court just declared Bothwell innocent of murdering anyone. *Her* court.

JAMES. And she thinks he is innocent!

And Bothwell has four thousand armed men around him, they walked with him to the court.

(*Losing it a bit.*) Christ I *telt* her! I warned her and warned her.

(*Collects himself.*) Well... she's ready to listen to me now. She listens to me and we're leaving that killer here in Edinburgh. The lords of Scotland are telling you to keep her here, for her own *safety*? Is that the line they're giving you? Locked up with a murdering bastard and an army four thousand strong? No. We're going to Stirling. She's left her son there, safe, with his nurses. We're going to put that bairn back in her lap. Her heir. Scotland's future. She can rule from Stirling as well as she can from Edinburgh. All you need to do is open the gate.

THOMPSON *says nothing*.

Thompson?

AGNES. Maybe we're no wanting a Catholic queen any mair.

JAMES. Aw will you *please* stop butting in! I mean seriously, I could *actually* stab you myself and they wouldny put me on trial.

AGNES. And she is a murderer. She hated Darnley. She wouldny stay under the same roof as the boy.

JAMES. Henry, Lord Darnley, was a big pisshead of a disappointment to us all. I'm no giving you an argument on that.

AGNES. She wanted rid of him so she could marry her dog.

JAMES. That's the story. Aye. Who put that about, do you think? Who'd like us all to have the idea he could marry a queen? Which grinning, mongrel cur would that be? And fiels like you believe it. I told her so. I told her what the likes of you were thinking. You should have seen the look on her face, the *disdain* at the idea she ruled a nation of folk daft enough to think she'd shag a jumped-up gutter rat like yon.

AGNES. Well, why else did she have Darnley killed?

JAMES. She never had him killed!

If you'd seen her… when she got the news…

She was visiting him that night. Why? Why would she visit a house with its basement stuffed full of gunpowder if she knew it was there?

She nearly stayed with Darnley that night. She was making her peace with him. She let him hold her hand and promised to visit him the next day. Ask anyone who was there! She might have stayed with him. She only left because she'd promised to dance at her friend's wedding.

You know what her first thought was? Once she took in that he was dead? 'They could have killed me too'… and they could. One thing we know, the gunpowder was already in the house when she was.

The fuse was already laid,

The killers were waiting in the streets around about.

She left the house just before midnight. The murderers must have watched her leave. Were they waiting for that? Did they care? She canny be sure. Why are you?

But some time after she left the doors to that house were locked, from the outside. No one inside could get out. Darnley maybe heard them then, looked out and saw the . murderers barring the door. He climbed out a back window before they blew the house but they caught him...

They caught him in the garden...

That was one of the happiest days of her life, the day before her husband was murdered. She danced at the wedding breakfast, spent her day talking and eating with the lords of Europe and then danced again, danced the last hour of the day away...

I've no seen her smile since.

A beat.

AGNES. Aw you've told that well. Poor wee Mary. I can just see it. So why is Darnley dead again? Did I miss that bit?

JAMES (*to* THOMPSON). Why is she no scared of me?
I canny mak it oot.

AGNES. Aye, you'd like us frightened, eh? You'd like to bully and terrify this poor boy into doing your bidding. And do you care if he's killed? You dinny seem to care much that he took a beating.

JAMES (*to* THOMPSON, *not her*). Darnley is dead because he stopped being useful. When she loved him the 'great lords' of Scotland could use him to pull her strings... but she soon saw him for what he was – a pox-ridden whining waster. She stopped listening to him. She could barely stand to be near him. Darnley's dead because he wasny useful any mair, but he still knew all their secrets. Of course they needed him out of the way. So those lords you're taking orders from turned their faces away and let a wild Bothwell beast go and do their killing. But *now* they canny get Bothwell back on his chain. Well, now they'll learn. They made the monster. Let it eat them all. But you and I need to protect the Queen.

AGNES (*to* THOMPSON, *urgent*). John. What's going on here? What have you heard me say?

THOMPSON. We can make a better world. A better Scotland.

JAMES. Lovely! On you go! Who's stopping you?!

AGNES. One where we don't have to give all we have to priests just to pass safe to heaven.

JAMES. And your Queen is *happy* about that! She's not...

AGNES (*cutting* JAMES *off*). We don't have to let someone else talk to God, in language we canny understand. We can just look up and speak to him straight. From my heart to the ear of God...

JAMES. She has the ear of *God*, well, you're right, I canny fucking compete wi' that.

(*To* THOMPSON.) It's gonny be carnage! Civil war! We have to get the Queen away!

AGNES. John Thompson, did you not see when you looked at me that I was looking back?

THOMPSON (*to* AGNES). I didny know you knew my name.

AGNES. I asked. Of course I asked.

She touches him.

JAMES. I've lost your attention now, eh? You've got God's own wee handmaiden, his voice on earth whispering in your ear.

Aye, we all saw the sense in the new religion, but answer me this...

AGNES *and* THOMPSON *are still focused on each other.*

Oy! You! Maidservant to the Lord! Answer me one thing...

What did you say when you saw the blood on the floor there? Can you remember? Did you hear yourself?

She doesn't answer.

'Mother of God.'

You called on Mary, Mother of God, just like the priests taught you from a bairn.

There are no good Protestants in this nation!

No yet. Your 'true' religion... *our* religion is just a thin skin on all that went before, scum on a puddle.

AGNES. Aye. *Aye!* The reek o' oor burning martyrs is still smoke in the air! We're only halfway saved. Which is why we need good men to lead us now.

JAMES. We do. Where are they? Show me. Point them out. You think those lords through there planning to imprison their own Queen are *good men*?! Do you?

Well, let me tell you something. The great lords you think defend you from popery only do it to keep their cash. They don't need to pay a tithe to Rome if they declare the Protestant faith, do they? All that money stays safe in their own fat purses.

Money.

That's their religion. Money and murder.

You want to see a good man? I'm *right* here. I share your faith, missus. *I share your Protestant faith!* But it doesny mak *me* a traitor.

(*To* THOMPSON.) And nor will you be, you just need to open the gate.

AGNES *is still talking to* THOMPSON.

AGNES. Bothwell and his kind are scum, alright, but they're better for Scotland than her! Keep the faith!

JAMES. Open the gate!

THOMPSON *is torn.* JAMES *and* AGNES *are now both focusing just on him.*

Listen, man, listen. This is a moment here, a moment that changes everything. This is history, this is what's going to say who you are, what Scotland becomes.

AGNES. Did she convert? No. What else matters?

JAMES. Do you want to be the man who ended the reign of three hundred years of royal Stuart blood? We're a nation that lives in argument but we've all chosen that blood to lead us through all our woes and wars for generations...

AGNES (*cutting in*). We're what Scotland becomes, John, you and me and those like us...

JAMES (*cutting in*). *Royal blood. That* unites us, it's the only thing that ever has.

AGNES. He's just trying to frighten you, don't listen...!

JAMES (*cutting in*). Do you want to close the gate in the face of our best hope of peace?!

THOMPSON *doesn't know what he should do*.

THOMPSON. I need to...

AGNES. Aye, you *know* what you need to do...

THOMPSON (*to both of them*). Let me think, will you?!

JAMES. Have you been to Europe? No?

I've seen sunset behind the Jura Mountains. Peaks of ice, lit up with light, great slabs of rock and snow like a staircase to heaven.

AGNES. Dear Lord. Don't let him start all this...

JAMES *turns on her. He might have a weapon*.

JAMES (*cutting over her, furious*). Something else to think about, Thompson! What do you think the other great lords of Scotland would do to a servingwoman that kept talking over them?!

AGNES *subsides in the face of his increased threat*.

Well, watch what I do, and then you can do a wee compare and contrast about who loves the peace of Scotland more.

(*To* AGNES.) I'll no hurt you but you need to be quiet now.

(*Gathering himself*.) Where was I?

Aye. In Italy. I've run through wars.

I've seen rivers and plains and deserts and forests that make everything you've ever seen look like a shabby garden full of weeds.

The friends who loved me in France were so angry when I said I was coming back to Scotland. They said I was throwing away my life.

Why would I throw away a life of wonders?

When I first saw Queen Mary she was standing by a fountain in the garden at Fontainebleau. She was nine years old. She smiled to see me. 'Are you from my Scotland?' she said.

You know the look she has? Such a little face on that long stalk of a body. You couldny say she was beautiful... but then you realise you've never seen anyone you wanted to look at more.

She had that, already, a smile that charmed and grabbed your heart straight away, a good but greedy bairn snatching up another sweet.

When she decided she was coming back to Scotland, to take up her throne – she asked to talk to me. She was excited. Frightened, aye, but ready for it. I've never seen her better, it was like she was lit up from inside.

'I'm Queen of Scots already, Melville, but I don't know Scotland. Will you help me? Will you advise me? I promise I'll always be guided by you. Will you tell me what's best for Scotland?' She was nineteen.

And that was the choice. I had a life of wonders, all the countries of Europe to roam through, the best friends a man can have in every corner of every kingdom... I was rich. I mean, proper rich, European rich.

Why would I come back here?

For her. For Mary. For Scotland. I couldny separate the twa. A Queen that wanted to love all her people. A country crying out for love and peace.

A lass that had had her fingers round my heart for ten years.

A country that first set that heart beating.

I came back for love.

That love makes me James Melville. It's who I am. It's all I am.

And that was the moment that made me. The moment I chose.

Son, this is the moment that'll make you. If the Queen's imprisoned then the Scotland that made us, that you were born into, is gone and we're in a world of war.

So just choose. But know what you're choosing. Know who you are.

THOMPSON *still hesitates.*

AGNES. John, in these four years, she never put down her rosary beads.

THOMPSON (*to both of them*). Stop it! Just stop it! Let me *think*!

He's struggling, thinking hard, completely torn. At last he looks at JAMES.

I'll go and speak to them.

I'll speak to my men on the gate.

JAMES. Good man. *Good man!*

THOMPSON *leaves.* JAMES *shows his complete triumph.*

AGNES *just watches as he gloats.*

AGNES. Aye. I saw your Mary. The Mary that walks in gardens.

When she first came back to us we threw flowers for her to walk on up from Leith. She was that young and fresh and that glad to see us.

And we were that glad to see her.

I *bought* Marguerites, biggier and bonnier than anything I could've picked in a foggy field. I threw them down and screamed a welcome at her. I thought she would be part of our new hope.

But I've seen her closer now. I know her better now. Whatever she says, we both know she wants us all Catholic again. Well, the poor folk o' this nation have been tricked and robbed and twisted by her Church long enough. No more.

JAMES. One day, I know this, one day, you'll say sorry. 'Sorry, Lord Melville, I did Queen Mary wrong, she didny deserve my ill-wishing.'

No, you don't believe me.

AGNES. Well... you love her. I believe that.

JAMES. Like I said. It's who I am.

She's about to leave. He stops her.

No. You're not running off to talk to anyone. You'll stay by me until the Queen's safe on her way to Stirling. Don't worry, I'll not bring you with us. You'll be locked up safe before we're even on the road.

AGNES. You can't lock me anywhere!

JAMES. There's still cellars and cages for thieves and murderers. And there's still some men who answer to me holding the keys to *those* gates.

AGNES. You'll not keep me locked up!

JAMES. You think? You think you'll be missed? Mebbe. All I know is after today I'll never have to look at you again. Come away from here. Come on. Move!

He bundles her off.

For a moment we see or sense Mary Queen of Scots moving through the space.

A Room in Holyrood Palace

The room is flooded with sunlight. THOMPSON *is looking out over a sunlit garden.*

This is June.

THOMPSON. Look at that, will you look at that? It's proper summer now, eh?

JAMES. Is this going to take long?

THOMPSON. I wouldny imagine so.

JAMES. I would like to get home today.

THOMPSON. You don't have a place in Edinburgh any more?

JAMES. No, no. I've never had a place of my own in town. I always stayed here in Holyrood Palace, of course.

THOMPSON. Well, we could put you up here, if it came to it.

JAMES. Are you saying I'll have to stay over?

THOMPSON. No, no, not at all. We can make this very quick.

JAMES. Alright then.

A beat.

Go tell him I'm here.

THOMPSON. Tell who?

JAMES. Regent Moray.

THOMPSON. Oh no! No, sorry, he wants me to talk to you.

JAMES *is taken aback.*

Sorry, did you no realise?

It's clear JAMES *didn't.*

Aye! Aye, it's just you and me, Lord Melville. Just like old times. Well... no that old, couple of months, eh?

A lot happened since then.

JAMES *says nothing*.

I brought this back for you.

(*Offering the handkerchief*.) It's been weel washed. No a mark on it.

JAMES. That's... You can keep it. I said you could keep it.

THOMPSON. Very good of you.

Much appreciated, my lord.

Where did you stay then? When you were at court? Here? The royal rooms?

JAMES. No.

THOMPSON. You had your own rooms?

JAMES. Yes.

THOMPSON. Whereabouts?

JAMES. In this part of the house.

THOMPSON. Oh you got the garden view! You fair have to throw your weight about to get the garden view, eh? Worth it though.

JAMES. Why am I here?

THOMPSON. Well, my master, Regent Moray, thought we should talk to you.

JAMES. About?

THOMPSON. Mary Stuart of course. Who else?

JAMES. The Queen?

THOMPSON. Is she?

JAMES. Is she what?

THOMPSON. The Queen.

JAMES. Mary Queen of Scots. The clue's in the name.

THOMPSON. That's what you think?

JAMES. That's simple fact.

THOMPSON. Well… that's what we're here to talk about.

He pushes documents towards JAMES.

JAMES. What's this?

THOMPSON. A written demand that Mary Stuart should abdicate her throne and let her son rule Scotland instead.

JAMES *stares at it, taking this in.*

And we'd like you to sign. We'd like her to see your name there.

JAMES *says nothing. He pushes the papers back towards* THOMPSON *and moves to leave.*

My lord, Regent Moray did want you to remain until he had an answer on this.

JAMES. Then tell him to come and ask me.

I haveny seen him properly since he got back from France. I should congratulate him.

(*Sarcasm.*) Got hame just in time to rescue the nation, eh? Great timing. Send him in to me and I'll shake his hand.

THOMPSON *doesn't answer.*

Fine. Well, I'm signing nothing.

JAMES *is on the move.*

THOMPSON. Can I ask why?

JAMES. Why I won't tell the Queen I've served, all my life, to step off the throne?

No, you tell me, you tell me, what grounds do you have to go against the laws of God and man and…?!

THOMPSON (*cutting him off*). She's out of control. Ruled by carnal lust. Driven by it to adultery, murder.

JAMES. You think I'll sign my name to *that*?

THOMPSON. I hoped you might.

JAMES. Why would you even imagine…?

THOMPSON (*cutting him off*). She brought war on us.

JAMES. She …

(*Falters.*) Aye… that's what it came to… once…

He trails off.

THOMPSON. Once she'd married Bothwell. Aye, naebody fancied that king, did they? She didny even look happy about it…

JAMES. Well, of course she didny!

THOMPSON. Why 'of course'?

JAMES *doesn't answer.*

The reason I think you'll sign this is that when Bothwell and Queen Mary gathered that pathetic wee army, to turn on her own people, you wereny at her side.

Were you?

JAMES. My loyalty is to my Queen and always will be.

THOMPSON. How was it looking on the high street, when you came in? Quiet, was it? Peaceful?

JAMES. Quiet enough.

THOMPSON. Because there was bloody murder near the Tron last night. No one knows if we've a queen or a king or what we've got. No one knows if there's a government of lords that'll stand together or if it'll be civil war till the last throat's cut. The crowd's barely cleared off the high street since we brought the Queen through the town.

JAMES. I heard about that. The men that were there told me what happened. That was handled very badly.

THOMPSON. Were there still women at the gate?

JAMES. What?

THOMPSON. Bunch of wifies off the Canongate. They've been screaming half the night, wanting to know what we're doing to Mary. These are the same wifies that were screaming she should be stoned as a hoor day before yesterday. Figure that

if you can. We need to shift them, wi' kicks and sticks if we
have to but, way things are, on the street, we canny risk that.
Folk need to see we've got peace before we start punishing
the ones breaking it.

It's a mess. If we don't get a hold on this soon there'll be no
end to it...

(*Re: the papers.*) That's what this is about. Keeping the peace.

He waits. JAMES *says nothing.*

My lord, I'm sure you can imagine, there'll be consequences
if I can't present your signature on that document.

JAMES. For you or for me?

THOMPSON. For both of us.

JAMES. Am I under arrest then?

THOMPSON. No... *no...* nothing that... immediate.

JAMES. Don't you threaten me! Don't you *dare...*!

You think I'll betray Queen Mary now? I was there! I know
what she went through...

THOMPSON (*cutting in*). I know what you've been saying.
Trouble is, I'm no sure it makes the best sense.

JAMES. I'm no explaining myself to you.

THOMPSON. Well, thing is, you need to. So I can explain it to
the Earl of Moray. I've been close adviser to his grace since
he came home from France.

Does that surprise you? That the Earl would turn to me?

(*Reads the answer.*) Course it does. Nae harm. Canny quite
believe it mysel.

Regent Moray I should say.

That's what we should call him, eh?

That's the correct title, for the ruler of Scotland. He's been
quite... concerned, about some of the things you've been
saying. Particularly what you've been saying about what
happened to the Queen at Dunbar.

JAMES. It's a truth that should be told.

THOMPSON. You're a man of principle. Aye. I felt that.

I thought we shared a lot last time we met, didn't you? I felt. I don't want to presume, but I felt I understood you that day, sir.

That's why I advised the Regent to let me talk to you.

I persuaded him that was best.

It's a great feeling, eh? When royalty takes your advice. Well, you'll know.

You accept he's royalty, don't you?

JAMES. What?

THOMPSON. Regent Moray. The ruler of Scotland. The Queen's half-brother. You accept he's proper royalty?

A nasty pause.

JAMES (*careful*). Yes.

THOMPSON. Because some folk call him a bastard.

Well, he is a bastard, eh? Technically. Well, any way you want to look at it. His father might have been James Fifth of Scotland but his mother was not that King's wife. He was a bastard. Born out of wedlock. But royal.

JAMES *says nothing*.

Royal enough for you?

It's just I remember you said that three hundred years of Stuart royal blood was important.

JAMES. He's the Regent, for now. No our king.

THOMPSON. True enough, true enough, an important distinction.

Well, he's allowed me to have this time with you, Lord Melville, to talk things through, together. And I believe I can make you see your way to signing that paper.

JAMES. No.

THOMPSON. That's a shame.

So... mebbe I should have showed you the whole document, my lord. This second page has the signatures we've gathered already.

He shows JAMES.

As you can see, most of the other lords have signed. It would be good to see your name there too.

JAMES *is reading*.

It's...

Well, it's a question of loyalty.

At this point.

JAMES. My loyalty is to Scotland and to the Crown and there's an end to it.

(*Re: the papers*.) If these... *gentlemen*... can twist their conscience to this then I hope they can sleep well.

THOMPSON. You know better, eh?

JAMES. Aye.

THOMPSON. You alone. Of all the great men in Scotland, you *alone*, know different.

He lets that hit.

Then you should tell us, tell me, what you believe. From what I've heard you've no been quiet about it elsewhere.

JAMES *says nothing, shaken by the list of names*.

It's just it's not a story anyone else is telling.

JAMES. As I said, every man has to answer to his own conscience. And mine won't let me sign.

AGNES *is on*.

THOMPSON. I've asked Agnes to step in to hear this. You don't mind?

AGNES. Good to see you again, my lord.

THOMPSON. She knows the Queen. She's got a woman's insight.

AGNES. I do.

THOMPSON. Is that alright?

JAMES *is taking in the implications of* AGNES*'s arrival.*

AGNES. You'll see some changes here, eh, my lord? Different hands hold the keys to the locks these days.

Don't mind me, I'm no really here.

THOMPSON. I'm going to suggest something to you, my lord. I'm going to suggest that all our present trouble, all the chaos and violence that threatens us now, had its beginning in that day at Dunbar.

JAMES. Aye. I'll give you that.

THOMPSON. So I know you were with her that day. The day I opened the gate. The day she went out of Edinburgh.

JAMES. Yes.

THOMPSON. So the Queen's household were all together, going to Dunbar...

JAMES. No.

THOMPSON. No?

JAMES. No we weren't going to Dunbar.

THOMPSON. My mistake. Where were you going?

JAMES. Stirling.

You know that.

THOMPSON. How many of you were there?

JAMES. Thirty, give or take.

THOMPSON. A crowd of you! So when he came at you, Bothwell, he came out the side road at Gogarburn, did he? Or was he already at the ferry?

JAMES. I didn't see.

THOMPSON. Came out of nowhere.

JAMES. That's what it felt like.

THOMPSON. How did he know you were going to be there?

JAMES. You'd have to ask him that.

AGNES. Good luck catching him now.

THOMPSON. So how many were alongside him?

More than you?

JAMES. Yes.

THOMPSON. His whole four thousand men?

JAMES. No that many.

THOMPSON. So you stopped.

JAMES. Well, of course we stopped.

THOMPSON. Why 'of course'?

JAMES. He stopped us. He stopped the Queen.

THOMPSON. How?

JAMES. He caught hold of her bridle.

THOMPSON. He rode up and stopped her horse.

JAMES. Yes.

AGNES. Why did she no scream?

JAMES. She'd mair dignity! I never heard her scream! Ever.
No even when…

   He breaks off.

AGNES. What?

   JAMES *doesn't reply.*

THOMPSON. Well, we'll get to that, eh?

I imagine we might get to that soon enough.

So he stops her.

JAMES. Aye.

THOMPSON. And you let him?

JAMES. We were outnumbered. They had weapons. Weapons ready.

THOMPSON. And you didny?

JAMES. No! I just told you. They came out of nowhere.

THOMPSON. You couldny defend her?

JAMES. She told us all to leave it.

THOMPSON. She told you to stand down, she was happy to go with him?

JAMES. She didny want us getting hurt!

THOMPSON. 'Leave it, boys, it's no worth getting hurt over this'?

JAMES. Something like that, aye!

AGNES. Doesny sound like her.

JAMES. That was her meaning.

THOMPSON. And then she went off with Bothwell?

JAMES. They took her away. Aye. And me with her.

THOMPSON. Why?

JAMES. Why what?

THOMPSON. Why did you go with her?

JAMES. There was an armed captain with a blade at my throat!

THOMPSON. Right enough, and you'd never got your weapon out, eh? Or she'd told you not to.

JAMES. That's right.

THOMPSON. But why do you think they wanted you along? And Huntly. And Secretary Lethington?

JAMES. We're…

(*Corrects himself.*) We were her closest servants.

THOMPSON. Closer than her women?

JAMES. They took them too.

AGNES. Everyone she needed to be comfortable, eh?

THOMPSON. Where was she? Beside you? Ringed in with all those sharp swords?

JAMES. Lord Bothwell kept her by him, at the front of the line.

THOMPSON. With a blade to her throat too?

A beat.

JAMES. I didny see.

THOMPSON. And they just took the Queen, you, Huntly and the Secretary Lethington. None of the rest.

JAMES. No.

THOMPSON. They let them go free?

JAMES. Yes.

THOMPSON. Now...

(*A little hesitant.*) Sorry, my lord, but, you should know... Lethington says there was no weapon near the Queen, or him, and he says he had an idea Queen Mary was expecting to meet Bothwell on that road.

JAMES. If she was she never told me about it!

Lethington's a...

AGNES (*cutting in*). She'd have told you, would she?

JAMES. She told me everything!

THOMPSON. Aye. Advised by you in all things, since she was a bairn. That's what you telt me, eh?

JAMES. She valued my advice. Yes.

THOMPSON. And you're a loyal man, you told us that. You gave up European riches for Queen Mary, eh?

JAMES. Yes.

THOMPSON. But you left her the day after she rode into Dunbar with Bothwell.

You were happy to leave her there, without your protection?

JAMES. I... I couldny do anything. Not alone.

THOMPSON. So she'd asked you to get help? She was in danger?

JAMES. Of course she was but...

THOMPSON (*cutting in*). Lethington says you asked her permission to leave and she gave it. Why would you ask her permission to leave, a loyal man like yourself, if she was in danger? Why would she let you go?

JAMES *says nothing*.

AGNES. I think that one knew fine well how to lie in the bed she'd made there.

THOMPSON. Lethington says she gave you her hand to kiss and she smiled.

She *smiled*.

'Go if you need to, Lord Melville, but I'm happy to stay.'

JAMES. She didny say that.

THOMPSON. She didny smile?

JAMES. They were looking at us, everyone was looking at us. If she was watched, she smiled, even if she was shaking apart inside. She always smiled. She was taught to do that in her cradle.

AGNES. I thought you said you never saw her smile again after they strangled poor wee Darnley.

JAMES *ignores* AGNES, *only talking to* THOMPSON.

JAMES. Christ, man, you know what I meant!

THOMPSON. So what did she say, that day, when you left?

JAMES. I don't remember.

THOMPSON. She said she was happy to stay.

That's what everyone else heard her say. And they were all looking at her, and her smiling.

JAMES. I already told you.

THOMPSON. Why then?

JAMES. What?

THOMPSON. Why did you ask to leave that day?

JAMES. She...

He can't speak for a moment.

There was nothing I could do!

It was too late.

I'd told her. Well, you know what I told her. When we left here... the day you opened the gate... she was done with him. She heard my advice. She understood, finally, what Bothwell was.

THOMPSON. She told you that?

JAMES. Aye.

AGNES. And you think she always told you the truth?

JAMES (*ignoring that*). And I told her that her friends would keep her safe.

Well, we didn't. Did we?

THOMPSON. Why? What did he do to her?

JAMES. You know. You *know*!

THOMPSON. Tell me.

JAMES. You've already decided what you want to believe! All of you! You've decided she went with Bothwell willingly when I'm telling you she did not, you've decided she stayed with him, willingly, when I've just told you she did not. You've decided she lay with him, willingly, when the truth is... the truth is...

THOMPSON. What?

JAMES. He raped her! Alright? Happy now? That what you wanted to hear?

THOMPSON. No. No, I'm not happy to hear that at all. Because if that's true, Queen Mary was brought so low it's a shame on our whole nation.

If that's true we stood by, every one of us, and watched our Queen marry a man that should have been burnt in front of her for treason.

If that's true we should all lie at her feet and beg her forgiveness for letting that treasonous bastard come within a mile of her, whatever road she travelled.

(*Re: the papers.*) If it's true this signed demand for her abdication is an insult and an injury.

If it's true there is no law or decency in the whole country.

JAMES. Well, it's true.

THOMPSON. Well, I hope it isn't.

JAMES (*bitter*). It's true and every lord that signed your paper knows it.

THOMPSON. You think?

What a pack of cowards, eh?

All the more reason to get to the bottom of this then. This needs to come out before the coronation.

JAMES. The coronation?

THOMPSON. Her wee baby James. James the Sixth of Scotland. His coronation's planned for this week, did you no get an invite?

A beat.

JAMES. No.

THOMPSON. I suppose they thought...

(*Pretends to consider.*) Well, like I said, this is about loyalty now, eh? Would you even serve the wee boy?

A beat.

JAMES (*careful*). If I live so long I hope to serve James Stuart, one day.

AGNES. I bet you do.

THOMPSON. Aye, because folk like you and me, we're *fucked* wi'oot royal favour, *eh*, Lord Melville? I mean... you've probably got a wee bit land... if they let you keep it.

Mebbe you shouldny have run awa frae all those European riches, eh?

But we can hope for better days, eh? Peaceful, prosperous days.

Bothwell's gone. The mad dog was driven out at last, wasn't he? But your Queen was beside him till he ran...

AGNES. And what does that tell you?

THOMPSON *turns on her abruptly.*

THOMPSON. Agnes, will you...

Just wheesht a minute, eh?

AGNES. I've no said anything these last ten minutes!

THOMPSON (*back on* JAMES). You see how it looks, Lord Melville? You told me, you kept telling me, that Bothwell was the scourge o' Scotland, the evil in the heart of our government. And then your Queen runs off wi' him...

JAMES. I just told you...

THOMPSON (*driving over him*). She *marries* him!

JAMES. What choice did she have after...?

THOMPSON (*driving over him again*). And when all the good lords of Scotland rise up against him – as you wanted, Lord Melville, as you told me so plainly they *had* to do – what does Queen Mary do? She stays beside him. She joins him as he tries to make war on her *own people*. You told me Bothwell murdered the King. Everyone believes that now. Everyone knows that's true now. So what are we supposed to think when a woman marries the man who killed her last husband? When she stays with him even when the whole nation rises against them?

JAMES. She'd no choice!

THOMPSON (*cutting in*). Do you think she's *fit* to rule? State she's in now?

JAMES *hesitates*.

You are a man of great experience, Lord Melville. You don't need a green loon like me to spell it out. If our Queen isny fit to rule then we are looking at chaos, an empty throne. We want to get that bairn sitting on it with strong royal men and women around him to keep him safe.

AGNES. Aye.

THOMPSON. We need unity.

AGNES. Aye.

THOMPSON. We need peace of mind.

AGNES. Peace.

THOMPSON. We need your signature.

AGNES. She fooled you. Can't you see it? Is it no plain enough?

THOMPSON. You need to speak up, man. Declare for Moray. You canny just be silent, your silence isny good enough now.

JAMES. I know what you want me to say. I won't say it. She was *forced*. She never loved Bothwell. She trusted his friendship, for far too long, aye… but those were terrible days, after the murder.

Her mind was… scattered.

THOMPSON. Because if she'd taken your advice, after Darnley was killed, she'd have sent Bothwell away from court?

JAMES. Aye…

THOMPSON (*cutting in*). But she didny. Christ, that must have annoyed you. You know, there's something that's ay bothered me, every time I think back to that day when you were certain I needed to open the gate...

You all really thought it was safer to head out onto the open road, where anyone could chase after her, any armed man with a fast horse? You'd no thought your Queen might be... attacked?

JAMES. No.

THOMPSON. She had no... apprehensions, once you were out on the open road.

JAMES. No.

THOMPSON. So you're saying the Queen had no fear of Bothwell?

JAMES. No I didn't say...

AGNES (*cutting in*). Did she smile at him?

JAMES. Who?

AGNES. Bothwell. I mean, now we're clear she was smiling. Was she still smiling at him?

JAMES. No! No she was not!

THOMPSON. Why're you asking that?

AGNES. Just curious.

She never smiled at him?

JAMES. No those last few weeks. No. Never.

THOMPSON. What's that telling you, Agnes?

AGNES. That she wasny frightened of him.

JAMES. *What?*

AGNES. If a man has a knife at your throat you better smile when he tells you to. Even if he doesny. They need to see your teeth are too soft for biting.

She gives a big fake grin.

THOMPSON. If she was raped, why didn't you stop it?

JAMES. How could I?

AGNES. You could have done something, surely.

JAMES. We were in his house! His men everywhere!

THOMPSON. Aye. You said.

JAMES. I wasny even in the room!

THOMPSON. So how do you know she was raped?

JAMES. I don't want to talk about this. I will not talk to *you* about this.

She's been shamed enough.

THOMPSON. You're right. The shame of that could kill a woman.

AGNES *snorts*.

AGNES. If her immortal soul bides up her fanny, aye.

THOMPSON. Christ.

A moment.

Sorry, Lord Melville.

AGNES. My soul bides where no man can touch it.

THOMPSON. Aye, well, I think Mary Queen of Scots might be made of finer stuff than you, Agnes. I'd think the shame of that might kill her.

JAMES. Aye! So keep your filthy words to yoursel and…

THOMPSON (*straight on* JAMES). So why's she no deid?

JAMES. A week after the wedding…

THOMPSON. Her wedding to Bothwell.

JAMES. Aye…

AGNES. When she held his hand. When she took her vows, willingly, before *God*.

THOMPSON (*warning*). Let me do my work, Agnes.

JAMES. *Aye!* After that she was with some of us who still loved her, she was quiet in a room with myself and Arthur Erskine. He'll tell you! We heard her say 'I'd like to drown myself. Or get me a knife, I just want to be dead.'

THOMPSON. But she's no. You think all she needed was a wee knife? Plenty to hand. Lord Melville, you see our problem? You want us to believe you're the Queen's loyal servant, a man who loved her since she was a bairn...

JAMES. You know nothing about my love for her, my loyalty.

THOMPSON. Well, I'm no a brave man, I'm not, but if a woman I loved like a sister, like a daughter, was getting raped, I like to think I might at least do a bit of shouting.

You did nothing?

JAMES. I...

THOMPSON. And when you came back to Edinburgh, the day after, the day she told you you could go, you told no one. You never asked for help. You never went round shouting on any of us to rise up and come and save our Queen...

JAMES. Save her? You'd be glad to see her dead. Wouldn't you?

THOMPSON. You don't know what I'd like, James Melville.

JAMES. I can imagine.

AGNES. Seems like you're imagining a lot of things.

When a woman looks like royal Mary she'll ay get more than her share of pity. It takes another woman to see through all that soft shimmer to the true face o' the girl, wipe the tears off her and see what's really in her eyes. I'm sure you canny believe she's twisted your heart and made you a doughy puppet in her soft white hands. But I'll tell you this, one day soon you'll know what I know already. She made a fool of you.

THOMPSON. Can I get on now?

AGNES. I'm no stopping you.

THOMPSON. So, as I said, I'm adviser to the ruler of Scotland. Quite a hike for a wee doorkeeper frae Fife in just a few months.

JAMES. You think?

THOMPSON. Don't you?

JAMES. Or are you still just a wee doorkeeper that canny even get a servant to be quiet when he asks her to?

AGNES *starts to react to that.* THOMPSON *puts up a hand to stop her, driving on.*

THOMPSON. You know what put me on the path? Do you mind what you said to me? The day we last met?

'This is history, this is what's going to say who you are, what Scotland becomes.'

Two things.

Two things.

Who *I* was.

What Scotland would be.

Clear.

Simple.

And I saw it plain.

I could be that man. I could be like you, a servant who rose to stand beside the throne. A man who could decide how Scotland should be and make that happen. *I could do that*, if I just took a moment, like you said, to see whose favour would serve me best.

So I went to the lords and I told them the Queen did want to leave Edinburgh, just like they'd thought. And I told them you'd ordered me to open the gate.

JAMES *can't speak.*

AGNES *is loving this, gloating.*

Well, as you know, they let her go.

That surprised me, I won't lie.

JAMES. You told them?! And they knew Bothwell was already out there. They *knew*!

THOMPSON. Well, you must have known too, Lord Melville.

JAMES. *What?!*

THOMPSON. I told you Bothwell left after he'd flattened me. Where did you think he'd go?

AGNES. Did you tell Mary he'd meet you on the road or did she know already?

JAMES. What are you...?

I thought he was still in Edinburgh! We were heading for Stirling. He came out of nowhere!

THOMPSON. Aye. You said.

So I told them she was leaving. I told them you'd asked me to open the gate and let her through. And... you need to hear this, Lord Melville... I think some of those lords mebbe did just want to keep her safe. Whatever you think.

I told them what you'd said. I told them you said they couldn't make a prisoner of their own Queen. You could see that made them think too.

'Hell mend her then,' says Morton. I think it was Morton, aye, he gave me the order. 'If she doesny want to stay under our protection let's see what kind of queen she can be without it.'

Well, we found out, eh?

I just opened the gate.

Maybe, knowing what you know now, you wish you'd given me a different order, eh? Because if she'd stayed in Edinburgh, Bothwell would never have got near her. Would he?

JAMES *can't speak.*

Well, that was my moment. They were all looking me. I was carrying messages between men of power, eh? You said I'd know the moment, when it came.

I'll no toot my own horn but that was only the start of it. You need to do the thing that gets you noticed, aye. But after that, once they've seen you, you need to scramble to show how valuable you can be. And I did, I have. And here we are.

And now I'm the man who can decide the fate of the great Lord Melville.

AGNES. Are you getting that?

THOMPSON *takes a breath, controlling himself.*

THOMPSON (*to* AGNES). Can you just... there's a flow to the conversation and if you keep cutting in...

AGNES. You telling me when to speak?

THOMPSON. No, I just...

AGNES. Me that taught you how to look a duke in the eye and talk so he listened?

JAMES. She can say what she likes. I've told you. I've told you everything.

THOMPSON. I still don't understand why you're so sure the Queen wasny willing.

Even from the start of your story, it doesny add up. I mean... it's a *long* road from Gogarburn to Dunbar though, is it no? Hours to find an escape. If you wanted to escape.

JAMES. Alright then. Alright. You think she tricked me?

AGNES. That or you're a liar.

JAMES *turns to her.*

JAMES. And you think you see her plain. You think you see what only another woman could see?

AGNES. I know it.

THOMPSON. Lord Melville, you don't need to waste your time justifying...

JAMES (*cutting him off*). No! No! She's so sure she knows what happened, eh? She's certain.

(*To* AGNES.) So you imagine it. Imagine what it was like, for her, for Queen Mary.

Go on! Imagine you're on that long road, with a man like Bothwell holding the bridle of your horse...

Put yourself in her head.

AGNES. I don't need to do that.

JAMES. I thought that was what you were here for.

AGNES. No. No, I'm here to help you see sense and do your duty to...

JAMES (*cutting in*). So humour me. Or is Queen Mary the sort of woman the likes of you could never understand?

AGNES. I've the same sense between my ears as that one. Mair.

THOMPSON. Agnes, just...

AGNES *checks him*.

AGNES. *He asked me to speak!*

They didny waste much time, eh? Way I heard it he was up her skirts five minutes after she stepped through his door.

JAMES *can't speak*.

You want me to tell you what most women I know think? What most folk believe?

Most folk think she didn't want it at the time but after...

After he'd actually shagged her the first time, she liked it then. Or she liked him then.

She married him, did she no?

JAMES. What choice did she have? Who could have helped her after that? Who defended her after that?!

AGNES. Well, no, we can see you didny...

JAMES. Then I'll defend her now! Whatever you do, you can threaten me, you can tempt me, you can hang me out that window till the crows eat me, you cannot make me speak lies against Mary Queen of Scots!

THOMPSON. Well, good! That's very, very good! No lies. So you arrived at Bothwell's castle in Dunbar.

JAMES. Yes.

THOMPSON. You rode in the gate, together.

JAMES. Yes.

THOMPSON. Then what?

JAMES. There was a… reception… a meal that…

AGNES. That was the very first thing you did? And all of you so 'terrified'? You went to eat? The very first thing, the minute you were in the castle?

JAMES. No! I changed my boots, I had a piss, what do you want to hear?

THOMPSON. You got comfortable, after the journey. Course you did. Where did they put you? Nice room, was it?

JAMES. What?

THOMPSON. Did you get the view this time?

JAMES. I was in with Maitland of Lethington and Huntly. And our servants.

AGNES. Cosy.

THOMPSON. What about the Queen? She was taken to a room?

JAMES. Yes.

THOMPSON. Bothwell's room?

JAMES. She was the Queen!

THOMPSON. A room to herself?

JAMES. Yes.

THOMPSON. Did it have a lock on the door?

A beat.

Now. Just so you know, I do actually know the answer to this question, but I'd like to hear what you say.

Did the Queen's room have a lock on the door?

JAMES. No.

THOMPSON. Good. We'll come back to that. So you got in, freshened up, then you all had dinner. Together? Everyone in the hall?

JAMES. Yes.

THOMPSON. How was it?

The food, how was it?

JAMES. I don't remember.

AGNES. I once had a lovely bit of haddock in Dunbar. Was it a Monday?

Never eat fish on Monday.

THOMPSON. Can you remember what day it was?

JAMES. No.

THOMPSON. It was a Tuesday.

AGNES. You'd have been safe enough then.

THOMPSON. We know all sorts of concrete, provable things about that day. Don't worry about that, Lord Melville. The facts are known. Nothing can change the facts. What we want to understand is what you believe they *mean*.

AGNES. And what you saw. With your own eyes.

THOMPSON. After dinner. What did you do?

AGNES. Play games? The sweeties came round?

THOMPSON. Was there dancing?

JAMES. No.

AGNES. No dancing.

THOMPSON. James Hepburn, Earl of Bothwell, did not twirl your Queen about the floor?

A beat.

Remember, Lord Melville, there are other witnesses. Several of them.

JAMES. Yes.

He pulled her up and made her dance.

THOMPSON. She wasny willing?

JAMES. She had no choice.

AGNES. He had a fruit knife to her throat, did he?

JAMES *says nothing*.

And was she smiling?

Did she smile at you? When she caught your eye?

JAMES *says nothing*.

I think she did.

THOMPSON. So do I.

AGNES. And that's different, eh? Smiling at Bothwell, that could be terror. Smiling at you... sounds like she was comfortable enough.

THOMPSON. Was she drunk?

JAMES. No! No, she was not drunk!

THOMPSON. She knew what she was doing?

JAMES. She had no choice about what she was doing.

THOMPSON. And what happened next?

What did Bothwell do next?

JAMES. He...

He kissed her.

THOMPSON. On the hand?

JAMES. On the mouth.

AGNES. While they were dancing?

JAMES. Yes.

THOMPSON. So she pushed him off.

JAMES *doesn't respond*.

She slapped him then?

AGNES. She bit his face?

THOMPSON. Did she just go on dancing with him?

AGNES. Smiling?

JAMES. No.

AGNES. She stopped smiling?

JAMES. Yes.

AGNES. How did she look at him? After he kissed her?

JAMES. I couldn't see her clear.

AGNES. But how would you describe the expression on her face?

JAMES. She had no expression on her face.

AGNES (*concession*). That could be fear.

THOMPSON. Did she miss her steps in the dance? Did she tremble? Did she call out?

JAMES. No.

THOMPSON. That, could be passion.

JAMES. No.

AGNES. How can you be sure?

JAMES. I know her thoughts. I can read them on her face.

THOMPSON. You just said you couldny see her face.

AGNES. So what was she thinking?

JAMES. She had no love for James Bothwell then.

THOMPSON. But you told us, you told us she thought he was a… what was it, Agnes?

AGNES. An ugly guard dog. A lovable, toothless bear.

JAMES. Aye well, she had very poor judgement sometimes!

A beat.

THOMPSON. Well. That answers all sorts of questions, eh?

They kissed. They went on dancing. And what did you do?

JAMES. I left the room.

THOMPSON. Aye, we know you did. We know.

So after this, it comes down to what you believe, not what you saw.

JAMES. And what I heard!

THOMPSON. What?

JAMES. I heard them.

THOMPSON. Go on.

JAMES. Some of our people followed me out the room. Some of them stayed with her...

THOMPSON. Many witnesses, I told you.

JAMES. I stayed close.

THOMPSON. Why?

JAMES. In case she called for me.

THOMPSON. Did she?

JAMES. No.

THOMPSON. So what did you hear?

JAMES. A...

(*Falters*.) I heard...

There was a roar.

THOMPSON. A roar?

JAMES. The men shouted.

And they went on shouting. As if they were playing the ball or, watching a fight or...

THOMPSON. Watching James Hepburn, Earl of Bothwell, grappling with Queen Mary.

THOMPSON. That's what happened?

JAMES. I don't know!

THOMPSON. You were outside the door.

Right outside the door. In case she called for help.

JAMES. Aye.

THOMPSON. And she never did.

JAMES. No.

THOMPSON. Were you there when she came out the hall?

JAMES. Aye.

THOMPSON. How did she look?

JAMES. She was calm. She stood straight and looked calm. She walked past me, I said 'Queen Mary, do you need me?'

She said, 'No, no thank you, Lord Melville, I'm tired. I'm just tired and needing my bed.' So she went up to her bed.

THOMPSON. And she stayed there, in that room for ten days. In a room with *no lock on the door*. She could have walked out any time she liked.

JAMES *says nothing*.

And the next day, when you left her, she made no complaint.

JAMES. She barely spoke.

THOMPSON. But she said she was happy to stay.

JAMES. No!

She said…

She said…

'So you're leaving me now, James.'

THOMPSON. And what did you say?

JAMES. I said I had to leave her, that day, but I'd see her again soon.

THOMPSON. And what did she say?

JAMES. She said, 'It's alright, James. I'm well content to stay now.'

So I took my leave of her.

THOMPSON. Well content.

AGNES. And you didn't fetch her help?

JAMES. She was past help.

(*Bitter, at* AGNES.) The likes of you were already calling her a whore on the high street.

AGNES. The likes of me, you take a look at yourself –

JAMES. That's enough!

I'm done. Do your worst.

THOMPSON. What?

JAMES. On you go. I've told you the truth. I canny change it. I'm no signing your paper. Tell the Regent. Tell the lot of them, take my land, lock me up, throw me in a leaky boat and send me to the bottom of the sea. Just get on with it.

THOMPSON. My lord... you need to understand...

JAMES. I understand we're done here!

AGNES (*to* THOMPSON). You didny tell it to me like that.

THOMPSON. Like what?

AGNES. You didny tell me it was in the hall. You didny tell me the men were shouting...

THOMPSON. What difference does that make?!

JAMES (*to* AGNES). Aye! You see now! You're starting to understand now, eh?

THOMPSON. Lord Melville, I think we're heading down the wrong path now. Let me just suggest a few things to you.

AGNES (*cutting him off*). John, we need to stop. We need to slow down a minute. This isny right.

THOMPSON. Agnes! Just...

AGNES (*cutting in*). She just sat in that room for ten days...

(*Working this out for herself.*) Might have taken her ten days to believe it had happened to her, eh? And if she fancied the dog, before he bit her, well... she'd come to think it was her ain fault.

JAMES. There you go! Imagine it! Imagine what it was like for her!

AGNES. Look, we need to slow down. We need to think about this, John...

THOMPSON. No! You need to get out of here and...

JAMES. Let her speak!

AGNES. This is why they're angry on the street. Now we're talking about it, now we're really picturing it... we need to stop, and really think about this because what came after... what they did to her...

THOMPSON. Queen Mary is safe. Queen Mary is being held, safe, for her own protection.

JAMES. A prisoner.

AGNES. I don't care where the stupid woman is now. I care about us. I care about Scotland!

JAMES. She is Scotland. *She is Scotland.* Our Queen. And look what we've done to her.

AGNES. Alright, I admit it, I didny know. I didny think, what it was like for her. I hadn't been told the whole story, had I?

THOMPSON. You think you should have been invited into the Privy Council to hear all the business of government?

JAMES. Let her tell you what she understands now.

AGNES. Alright. I can see it now. She may have married the bastard but no, she probably wasny willing. So...

JAMES. So?

AGNES. Everything that came after starts from that. And I saw what came after. I was there.

  I thought we were building a new Protestant Scotland here. And I thought that meant an end to lies. That's what they do, you know, papists, they lie. For centuries they've told us the only way to heaven is through the gate a priest builds for you. And they've made us pay and pay and pay for that journey. They've made us all poor with their lies and soiled us all with their corruption.

JAMES. Queen Mary never defended men like that. She only wanted to keep her own faith.

AGNES. Aye, aye I'm no stupid. I know for every priest or bishop that whored and drank and robbed there was another who truly tried to love God, so what ruined the Church we had before? Lies. It was those lies. They twisted even those with pure hearts. Doesny matter if you truly tried to love God, those lies left us all standing in muck and greed and shame when we should have felt his glory.

  But now I'm thinking... how is this any better?

  We canny build the whole new nation of Scotland, a new church, a new faith on another lie. Can we? What'll happen to us if we do?

JAMES. There you go. But if the Queen can keep her truth, keep her dignity...

AGNES. Jesus. How could you do it to her? How could you just leave her there, like that? You *loved* her?

  And *now* you're wandering about whispering about what really happened to her?! What's the point of saying it *now*?

  (*To* THOMPSON.) You should have told me...

  (*To* JAMES.) And I think this is on you.

  It is, you know! Everything that came next is on you!

JAMES. And you! And the whole mob of you, wishing her dead... or worse.

AGNES. But you were *there*. You knew what he'd done to her.
Then you just kissed her hand and left her there? You
betrayed her.

THOMPSON. Alright, we need to get back on the right path
again...

AGNES. What do you think she saw on your face, James
Melville? That she was ruined, that she was shamed, that even
those that loved her couldny bear to look at her any more.

THOMPSON. Lord Melville, you've not betrayed her here or
anywhere.

JAMES. It was too late! I couldny save her.

AGNES. Why not? Why could you no go through that door?!

JAMES. Because I was afraid!

THOMPSON (*cutting her off*). Agnes, shut up now!

You need to get out of here.

Just get out of here. Off you go. Go and talk to the folk at the
palace gate then, the mob on the Canongate, on the high
street, all those folk that hang on your every word.

AGNES. And tell them what?!

THOMPSON. That we can have a true, Protestant monarchy at
last. Isn't that what you ay promised us all?

AGNES. I'll tell them what serves Scotland's peace. But I've no
heard it. When you asked me to come and help you I thought
our duty was clear. But now I've listened to him, now I've
thought about it.

It's not right, John.

Whatever she was...

THOMPSON (*cutting in*). We agreed *I* would talk to Lord
Melville! We agreed you would just listen unless I needed
you to speak.

AGNES. Or you needed to hear me. Well, you need to hear me...

THOMPSON. I should never have let you in the room.

AGNES. We talked about this, last week…

THOMPSON. Have I been in your bed this last week, Agnes?

> Have you no seen where I've been spending my days? At Regent Moray's shoulder, every moment.

> See what everyone knows, Agnes, what everyone can see, is that right now the wheel is spinning so fast, *so fast*, that you need to run to keep your feet on it.

AGNES. And who put your feet on the wheel?

THOMPSON. Aye, you were a help to me, you were useful then. I won't deny it but you've no the sense to keep quiet when you're no use at all, have you? So why don't you get on your road?

> *She doesn't move, stunned.*

> Go on!

AGNES. Who do you think you're talking to, boy?

> Alright then. We are done. We are *done*.

THOMPSON. No quite. Apologise to Lord Melville.

AGNES. For what?

THOMPSON. You've insulted his honour and his courage and I don't want to hear any more of it. Apologise to his lordship!

JAMES. There's no need for that.

THOMPSON. You've got a soft heart, a soft heart when it comes to women. I can see that.

> (*To* AGNES.) I have one job to do here, Agnes. You were supposed to help. I thought you might help. Well, you didny. So we're done. And don't call me 'boy', ever again.

> Now gies a smile and get out the door.

> No smile?

> (*To* JAMES.) Apparently that means she's no scared of me.

(*On* AGNES, *vicious.*) *Well, you fucking should be!*

AGNES *leaves.*

THOMPSON *is seething for a moment.*

You know what I'm realising, Lord Melville? You know what I'm guilty of? Poor judgement! Very poor judgement.

Why would I make a mistake like that?

JAMES. You tell me.

THOMPSON. I'd've said I loved her. If we're being honest.

Doesny mix, does it? Statecraft and true love.

JAMES. No.

THOMPSON. There you go. Common ground.

Never mind Agnes, don't give her another thought. Just listen to me for one moment.

The men that were in the room with the Queen and Bothwell, the men that saw what happened *all* say she was willing. All of them.

JAMES. Aye, well they would.

THOMPSON. Why? They wereny all Bothwell's men, were they? This is my question. You didny see what happened. You were outside the door.

JAMES. Aw Jesus...

THOMPSON. No! Forget what Agnes said! Just listen a minute. Is it possible, is it *just* possible, that you're wrong.

Is it possible that she was willing?

Is there no even a *shred* of a chance that's true?

You saw nothing, *nothing*. You saw her smile. You saw her dance. Afterwards, you heard her tell you she was content...

You just need to *tell* me, man. You need to explain it to me, why are you so sure she was raped?

Folk that were in the *room* are no saying that!

JAMES. Have they got a better explanation?

THOMPSON. They saw him up her skirts, aye! But she was willing!

JAMES. They're all saying that? All of them?

THOMPSON. Every man that was in that room.

JAMES. I can't imagine how they can say that.

THOMPSON. Unless she was willing! Think about it… was it no the Queen hersel that put the idea he could have her in his head? Everything that happened to her after came from that! She kissed the wrong murderous wee scumbag, she let the wrong ambitious little traitor squeeze her tits.

JAMES. Don't you talk about her like that!

THOMPSON. Alright.

Excuse me. I'm sorry. But it makes me angry, my lord. What she did to Scotland. What she's done to you.

JAMES. To me?

THOMPSON. You tried to warn her. She wouldny be told. Am I wrong?

You say she told you everything, you say, time was, she took your advice in everything. But did you really advise her into everything that happened to her these last years?

JAMES. No! Of course I didny…

THOMPSON. So when did she stop listening to you?

When that wee monster Bothwell started turning her head. Am I right?

JAMES. Maybe before that.

When she was ruled by her heart…

Too often, she was ruled by her heart.

THOMPSON. Aye. Even Darnley! I mean he was her choice at the end of the day! How did you say it? 'A big pisshead of a disappointment to us all.' Do you think he was ever fit to sit beside her on the throne of Scotland?

No seriously, man, I'm just asking now.

Do you?

JAMES. No.

THOMPSON. I mean I'm no saying we've always had the best
kings but wi' *her*? Who was she going to drag up the aisle
next?

THOMPSON *shows* JAMES *the signatures on his papers.*

Look at the names, Lord Melville, half the lords in the
parliament! They agree with you. They all think she was led
astray by her own heart. But none of them think she was
raped.

You told me the facts, we just looked at them together, and
I still don't believe it.

JAMES *is looking at the names again, reading them.*

I understand you blame yourself. I can see that. It's a credit
to you. It's a reflection of your deep love for the Queen
but… man, you like to beat yoursel up, eh?

Can I tell you what I see, when I look at you?

A man who I look up to.

A man who inspired me.

And now you need to think about what's best for Scotland.

JAMES. It's not for the likes of you to tell me that.

THOMPSON. Alright. Maybe it isny! So you tell me. You tell
me, my lord. What should happen now? Could you put the
Queen back on the throne? Now?

And if not what happens? Civil war?

JAMES. So you and your *masters* want me to slander her, to
deny her, to make a peace you canny keep.

THOMPSON. I'll only ask you one more time, my last question
if you like. Can you honestly tell me that you were *certain*,
with every part of you, when you heard the noise from the hall
that you were hearing Queen Mary being forced? *Certain?*

JAMES. Alright. Yes… I hesitated…

THOMPSON. Aye.

JAMES. I wasny sure. In the moment…

THOMPSON. No! No! Because if you'd been *sure*, you'd've been straight through that door.

JAMES. But afterwards, I was certain.

THOMPSON. I'll say it again, witnesses, *many*, *many* witnesses *swore* she was willing.

JAMES. I don't want to believe that of her.

THOMPSON. And there it is. There. It. Is. You don't want to believe it, and you've held that faith for all these months.

Held it when she wouldny hear the truth about Bothwell.

Held it while she married him.

Held it when she tried to bring war on every man that wouldny close his eyes to what she'd come to. It's time to let that faith go. Because the truth is she let us down. Didn't she?

Right now we are a shattered kingdom that canny unite behind a ruler. A broken beehive full of buzzing, wi' no defence from greedy snouts snuffling at the honey.

You know all of Europe is looking at us? *England* is looking at us and they definitely know the way over our border with an army.

So what story should a man who loves Scotland, who loves peace, be telling the world now?

That we stood by while our own monarch was attacked?

And when King James is crowned…

JAMES. Who has the prince now?

THOMPSON. The wee King James?

JAMES. He's no that yet though, is he? Who has him?

THOMPSON. He's safe, in Stirling.

JAMES. Safe? If any one man holds him they could be ruler of Scotland.

The boy's barely making words, he won't have a thought of his own for years. He's a raw scone. You could stick your hand on him and make him any shape you wanted. God help Scotland. What will he become with men like you to advise him?

THOMPSON. Why shouldn't it be a man like you that advises him?

A beat.

JAMES. What are you saying, now?

THOMPSON. Yes, we have a baby king, pure in the new faith, unformed, ready to be guided by strong men, men who know what's good for Scotland, *good* men.

I think you're a good man, James Melville. I do.

JAMES. Well. Thanks for your opinion. What does Regent Moray think?

THOMPSON. As I said he's asked me to talk to you.

We were thinking... you've been to England before, many times, eh? It would reassure everyone, we think, if a man like yourself, with your experience, were to carry our messages down to the court in London.

JAMES. Ambassador to England?

THOMPSON. You've family there, eh? And you know Queen Elizabeth, don't you? She knows you, and she knows you loved her sister, Queen Mary.

JAMES. Why aren't you asking Lethington?

THOMPSON. I've tested your loyalty, and I've tested his, here, in this room. And now I'm asking you.

JAMES. Not him?

THOMPSON. No. You. We think Queen Elizabeth will hear the truth from you. You could tell her this is no rebellion. There's no disorder here, no chaos, no armed mob howling to take a royal woman's blood. Tell her no queens were raped to make this new Scotland.

JAMES. I don't need to be told what to say to Queen Elizabeth.

THOMPSON. I just meant…

JAMES. Wait.

(*Thinks*.) Queen Mary was seduced by an evil man. She was forced…

(*Corrects himself*.) She made a marriage that dishonoured her royal blood…

THOMPSON. Against advice…

JAMES. Mebbe…

Despite advice, she found herself with no choice but a marriage that dishonoured her royal blood. A marriage that destroyed the peace of Scotland.

THOMPSON. But we're loyal to her heir, King James.

JAMES. But all are loyal to her heir. King James.

THOMPSON. Her Protestant heir. England needs that security.

JAMES. The Stuart line continues. Peace will return.

JAMES hesitates.

THOMPSON. So you'll do it?

He pushes the papers towards JAMES.

A moment.

JAMES. You only once asked me the right question. The question is not why I didny go back through the door. The question is why I left the hall in the first place.

THOMPSON. You said you couldny stand to see her with him.

JAMES. I never could.

One second. One second when I hesitated, when I wasny sure. Why wasn't I sure?

THOMPSON. Like you said. She ay smiled at him.

JAMES. One time...

We were going through letters, all urgent stuff. He comes swaggering in and he pits his hands on her. *He pits his hands on her!* Took the pen away, pulled her up and took her off the go hunting. And she...

She saw my face. She says, 'Oh don't scold me, James, can't I have any fun at all?'

Oh aye. He was great fun. Earl Bothwell.

THOMPSON. Famous for it.

JAMES. But she...

It was still...

I canny forget what I heard... through that door.

THOMPSON. Save it for the memoir.

Lord Melville, now, right now, Scotland needs you.

Another moment.

Then JAMES *signs.*

Oh good man. Good *man*, James!

JAMES. I'm Scotland's man, no yours.

THOMPSON. Of course, Lord Melville. Sorry.

JAMES. I should see the Regent.

THOMPSON. He's waiting upstairs for news of this conversation. I'll take you to him.

JAMES. I need to wash. I need better clothes, my bag...

THOMPSON. Of course.

(*Elated.*) Lord Melville, sir, what a pleasure and a privilege to share another moment like that with yourself! I could feel the future shaping round us like great rocks sliding doon the hill to turn the course of a river.

Could you feel it?

Ach but that's nothing to a man like you, eh? Making history every time you walk into a room. It's like a dance, eh? Or swordplay. You've just got to go on instinct. You don't even know yoursel what you might use…

(*Can't keep it in.*) I told them I could turn you!

I'm just glad, so glad, we found our way to each other this time, Lord Melville.

JAMES *doesn't respond.*

I'll go to the Regent.

THOMPSON *leaves.*

After a moment, AGNES *comes in with a bowl of water.*

AGNES. I heard you needed a wash.

JAMES *won't speak to her. She puts the water down.*

JAMES *is getting on with cleaning himself up.*

I'm going to tell you something. I'm going to tell you what happened when they brought Queen Mary back into Edinburgh.

JAMES (*doesn't care*). Say what you want.

AGNES. I was watching when they brought her back through the town. After she surrendered to them.

We *shouted* her guilt at her. She was no queen then. She wasny smiling then. A crumpled grubby creature in just her petticoat, the tart.

'Burn her! Burn the whore! She's no fit to live!' And the men riding either side of her, all the soldiers bringing her in, they were shouting it too. 'We'll drown you, bitch. We'll run you through, you faithless cunt.'

Her face.

JAMES. Alright, that's enough.

AGNES. But you need to hear me. You think you know the worst that happened to her? What if I tell you there was mair?

I suppose she thought they'd bring her back here, to her palace. But they didny. A palace is for a queen and she was no queen then. They took her to the provost's house on the Canongate.

We saw them all come and go through the door, the lords of Scotland, and a wee while later, we saw her at the windy.

JAMES. No. You be quiet! That's not what happened! I heard this story. This *lie*! This is the mob speaking, folk like you that want to see her broken altogether. She was being held for her safety, from folk like *you*. The men that were there promised me...

AGNES (*cutting over him*). 'The men that were there'? 'The *men* that were there'?! I was there! I'm telling you what I saw with my own eyes, Lord Melville!

That checks him.

Somehow she'd got herself to the window of that house. She leaned out the window and she *screamed*!

'Help me! Help me! Look what they're doing to me!'

Lord Melville, her tits were out. Her whole petticoat was ripped and her tits were out. *Screaming!* And then they pulled her back in.

JAMES (*trying to push this away*). No...

AGNES. Some folk laughed.

Someone said, 'Christ, she must fair be missing Bothwell, she's tearing her claes off she's that desperate for another shag.' And folk laughed harder. I laughed. Though I didny think it was funny.

JAMES. I don't believe this. I won't.

AGNES. Lord Melville, think about it. She was hanging out the windy with her hair all over the place and her tits out! The Queen of Scots! Screaming. 'Look what they're doing to me!'

You didny see her raped in that room in Dunbar Castle but you *know* she was. You didny see this but you *know* how half the men of Scotland looked at her. How *you* looked at her. What did you think would happen when her royal power was gone and they had their hands on her? What did you think they'd do?

JAMES. Better than you that hated her!

AGNES. Right enough. I just watched. I told myself I wasny sure about what I was seeing. But now... I'm certain.

A lot of the other women went and started hammering on the door of that house.

'What are you up to in there?! Leave her alone! Leave Queen Mary alone!' They kept hammering and shouting till the men brought her out in a clean dress. Those women waited till they heard her say she was – 'Fine, thank you, fine'... that's what I think she said, voice just a wisp of nothing.

Then the men took her away to her prison. And God knows what else they're doing to her there.

We're the same, you and me. You stood outside the door and wouldny go in.

I stood on the street and didny go near the door either.

But we both know, aye? We both *know* when you say it back, it's clear. She was raped.

And likely mair than once.

And that has to be talked about before this new nation can be whole... can be clean. Or what will happen to us?

He's not reacting.

Lord Melville?

There's a crowd of women still out there shouting to know what we've done to that lassie. They should be answered.

Still nothing.

I'm going to prove you right. You said I'd apologise one day... Are you hearing me? Sorry, Lord Melville, I did Queen Mary wrong, she didny deserve all my ill-wishing. I canny save her now. But you can. You can tell them the truth. We have to start with truth...

THOMPSON *is back on, hearing the end of this.*

JAMES (*to* AGNES). None of this is truth.

AGNES (*cutting in*). I was *there*! And I hate her! Why would I want to save the hoor unless the soul of Scotland was at stake?!

Tell them! You sit in parliament. Shout it there! Tell the Queen of England. Tell the world! Write it down and let the world know! You love her, you know what she felt what she thought...

Suddenly JAMES *turns on her.*

JAMES. *She thought he was her pet dog!!*

She was warned, but she wouldny hear it.

She loved him better than me!

Well. See where it ended.

A moment.

THOMPSON. You've a great heart, Lord Melville. It's terrible to see it break. But you're right. The fall of Mary Queen of Scots is a tragic necessity. There's no other way to reach peace now.

AGNES. That's a *lie*! Will you just...

THOMPSON (*cutting her off*). Agnes, you'll no be needed here after tonight.

You'll be leaving the palace. Your service is no longer required.

A beat.

AGNES. I'll no be quiet.

THOMPSON. No one wants to hear you any more. No one who matters. No one wants to believe you. And if they do... you'll be sorry. That's the truth.

AGNES. Oh aye. We all know that truth.

JAMES. My coat.

THOMPSON. Give his lordship his coat.

AGNES gives it to him.

AGNES. You said you couldny choose between the twa, Mary or Scotland. You said it was the love that made you who you are.

Who are you now, James Melville?

JAMES. An officer of the Scottish Crown.

He's moving away.

We see JAMES waiting/preparing to meet the Regent.

We hear WOMEN on the street. Then we see them. We see the street. More and more WOMEN, thronging onto the street.

The WOMEN are banging on the gate. 'What're you doing? Let us in. Where's the Queen? Tell us what you're doing to her? No more lies! No more lies!' … etc.

Then the shouting and the banging become unified. The WOMEN are all banging the gate together. They're all shouting together.

WOMEN. Let us in! Let us in! Let us in!

They freeze.

We just see JAMES, alone.

He hasn't moved.

He hasn't turned or looked at the WOMEN…

Mary is in his imagination. She walks up to him, looking at him, wearing just a red petticoat. She speaks to him, soft, sad.

MARY. Will you help me? Will you advise me? I'll always be guided by you. Will you tell me what's best for Scotland?

He holds her gaze a moment then turns away from her and she's gone. We just see JAMES. We see that he's close to breaking down.

www.nickhernbooks.co.uk

facebook.com/nickhernbooks

twitter.com/nickhernbooks